Wall Street: The History of the New York City Block that Became America's Financial Center

By Charles River Editors

Wall Street in the late 19th century

About Charles River Editors

Charles River Editors provides superior editing and original writing services across the digital publishing industry, with the expertise to create digital content for publishers across a vast range of subject matter. In addition to providing original digital content for third party publishers, we also republish civilization's greatest literary works, bringing them to new generations of readers via ebooks.

Introduction

A 1909 depiction of the NY Stock Exchange

Wall Street

"Wall Street is the only place that people ride to in a Rolls Royce to get advice from those who take the subway." - Warren Buffett

In the heart of Lower Manhattan lies a prestigious strip running 8 blocks long. From Broadway to the East River, impressive towers and columned buildings slapped with smooth, well-aged limestone stand proudly under the afternoon sunlight. Some of the nation's largest investment firms and brokerages line these blocks, and among these landmarks is one that effortlessly stands out from the rest: the home of the New York Stock Exchange. Resting on 11 Wall Street, this handsome curved structure built with white Georgian marble is a double-sided beaut. Above 3 flags rustling in the breeze, the Broad Street entrance boasts 6 Corinthian columns and is topped off with a triangular pediment featuring a sculpted series of human figures.

This distinguished district, of course, is none other than Wall Street. Smartly dressed men and women armed with swinging suitcases, phones, and Bluetooth headsets pour out of the buildings, joining the bustling crowd in the sidewalks. A few blocks down, tourists surround a gleaming bronze bull for a snapshot with the famous monument. All over the place, there is a palpable sense of urgency, determination, and fast-paced energy hanging in the air. It is an energy the driven inhabitants live, breathe, and thrive on each day.

Since the beginning of time, money and trading have shaped the economy of civilization. The earliest societies began with barter, otherwise known as the mutual exchange of goods and services. Grains, plant products, cattle, camels, sheep, and other livestock were the first forms of currency. In Eastern and African countries, money came in the likes of cowrie shells. Currency evolved as time progressed, passing through the ages as primitive copper coins, stamped coins, leather squares, stringed beads, gold, and finally, to the paper and electronic currency used today.

Back in the day, those who owned the largest fleet of livestock and farmlands climbed were at the top of the financial ladder. By today's standards, wealth is often measured by annual income, property, assets, and stock ownership. This most likely explains why many are so drawn to Wall Street, particularly to the NYSE, the world's largest stock exchange. Every year, thousands of young go-getters fresh out of college aspire to join the ranks, all to grab just a sliver of the pie Wall Street serves. And what a rich, hearty pie it is indeed; the market capitalization of the companies listed in the NYSE alone was at a reported $18.3 trillion in 2015.

Over the years, Wall Street has been equally glamorized and demonized for what it represents. To some, this is where lifelong dreams of riches, power, and fast living come to meet. To others, it is the breeding ground of the crooked 1%. All the same, its mystique is one that only the most ambitious penetrate.

Wall Street: The History of the New York City Block that Became America's Financial Center dives into the fascinating birth and history of Wall Street, as well as how it transcended through the years to earn its status as the world's leading trading hub. Along with pictures of important people, places, and events, you will learn about Wall Street like never before.

Wall Street: The History of the New York City Block that Became America's Financial Center

About Charles River Editors

Introduction

Chapter 1: Wall Street Before Wall Street

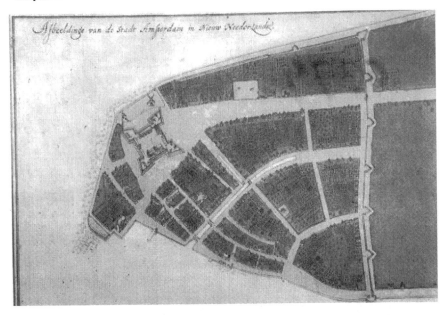

A colonial map of New Amsterdam

Wall Street has become a ubiquitous reference to the financial markets that call it home, but the name of the street itself provides a perfectly apt reference to its original use.

Manhattan has long been part of a bustling community, even before it formed the backbone of New York City. Centuries before New York City became a shining city of steel that enthralled millions of immigrants, Lenni-Lenape Indians, an Algonquin-speaking tribe whose name means "the People," lived in what would become New York, New Jersey, and Pennsylvania. They had lived there for at least 1,500 years and were mainly hunters and gatherers who would use well-worn paths that would one day bear the names of Flatbush Avenue, King's Highway, and Broadway.

The first known European sightings of the island and its inhabitants were made by the Italian explorer Giovanni da Verrazzano in 1524 and by the black Portuguese explorer Estaban Gomez in 1526. After the Englishman Henry Hudson, under the aegis of the Dutch East India Company, sailed by Manhattan in 1609, he returned home with good news and bad news. Like the other explorers before him, he hadn't been able to find a water route to the Orient. He had, however, returned with maps (confiscated by the British) and beaver pelts. With that, it became clear that the region around the bay that would take Hudson's name was a very promising new territory for trade and settlement, which would become a serious bone of contention between the Dutch and the British for the rest of the century.

In 1614, another East India merchant, Adriaen Block, entered through the narrows of the East River between Queens and Randall's Island, a difficult and dangerous passage that later sank numerous ships and that Block named Hell's Gate (Hellegat). The European world would know the name "Manhates" when Block returned to the Netherlands with new and improved maps. After that further exploration, the Dutch returned to build settlements on the southern tip of Manhattan and elsewhere, and by 1626 trade was brisk both between the Native Americans and the European settlers and between the settlers and their mother countries.

1626 was also the year that the famous "purchase" of Manhattan took place, a transaction for which no record has survived. Peter Minuit, the Director-General of New Amsterdam, paid out sixty guilders' worth of trade goods like cloth, kettles, tools, and wampum—an amount that's come down in history as being worth $24. While that sounds perversely low today, accountant types like to speculate with this amount, if the Lenni-Lenapes had invested it at a 10% interest rate over the centuries, it would today be worth $117 quadrillion—enough to buy present-day Manhattan many, many times over.

Many such purchases took place, but because Native Americans and Europeans had very different concepts of what it meant to "own" or "sell" land, misunderstandings—and violence— would frequently break out on both sides. Minor (and often unsubstantiated) thefts of property could ignite the colonists' wrath, resulting in such bloody skirmishes as the Pig War (1640) and the Peach Tree War (1655), named for the items allegedly stolen.

When the West India Company, which presided over Dutch trade in the Americas, was created in 1621, the little settlement at the tip of Manhattan began to both grow and falter. When Willem Kieft arrived as director in 1638, it was already a sort of den of iniquity, full of "mischief and perversity," where residents were given over to smoking and drinking grog and beer. Under Kieft's reign, more land was acquired mostly through bloody, all-but-exterminating wars with the Native American population, whose numbers also dwindled at the hands of European-borne diseases.

The Dutch tried to maintain good relations with all of the tribes for the sake of healthy trade but found themselves in the middle of conflicts among some of them, conflicts exacerbated by the fur trade. At Ft. Orange on the upper Hudson River, the powerful Mohawks of the Iroquois Confederacy challenged the Mahicans for access to the Dutch traders and attempted to become the middlemen with more inland tribes, so the Mahicans were forced to cede their land and relocate to the eastern side of the river.

In time, Indians who lived closer to New Amsterdam felt uncomfortable because the Dutch at

Ft. Orange had traded guns to their Mohawk enemies while they still had none to defend themselves. An additional factor causing Indians discomfort was the depletion of the fur-bearing animals with which they could trade for the commodities upon which they had become dependent.

As Dutch populations grew and expanded, the Indians became increasingly upset. By 1640, the Dutch had spread out from Manhattan and established new settlements on Staten Island, Long Island, and in the Bronx, which was named for Jonas Bronck after he settled there in 1639. They also settled in what is now Westchester County and New Jersey.

In September 1639, the relatively new director of the colony, Willem Kieft, set in motion a chain of events that led to warfare between the Dutch and some of the Lenni-Lenape around New Amsterdam when he demanded the Indians pay a tribute consisting of wampum, furs and corn. The 19th century historian, John Romeyn Brodhead, observed that this move on Kieft's part, which made sense from his point of view as a tax for services rendered by the Dutch to the Indians , understandably caused very strong ill feelings among the Indians. "They wondered how the sachem at the fort dared to exact such things from them.' 'He must be a very shabby fellow; he had come to live in their land when they had not invited him, and now came to deprive them of their corn for nothing.' They refused to pay the contribution, because the soldiers in Fort Amsterdam were no protection to the savages, who should not be called upon for their support; because they had allowed the Dutch to live peaceably in their country, and had never demanded recompense; because when the Hollanders, 'having lost a ship there, had built a new one, they had supplied them with victuals and all other necessaries, and had taken care of them for two winters, until the ship was finished,' and therefore the Dutch were under obligations to them; because they had paid full price for every thing they had purchased, and there was, therefore, no reason why they should supply the Hollanders now 'with maize for nothing;' and, finally, said the savages, because, 'if we have ceded to you the country you are living in, we yet remain masters of what we have retained for ourselves.'"

Kieft

Ultimately, warfare broke out in 1640. The Raritan band of the Lenni-Lenape were blamed for killing some pigs belonging to white settlers on Staten Island – white settlers typically let their swine run at large to forage in the woods -- although other evidence points to some servants of the Company as being the real culprits. Kieft decided that this was the right moment to show the Indians who was boss; he sent his secretary with a party of soldiers and sailors to demand reparations from the Indians and, if that were not forthcoming, to take as many of them as possible prisoner and destroy their corn fields. As a result, Dutch soldiers killed several Indians and took prisoner the brother of the sachem, and one of the soldiers on the boat back to Manhattan used a split piece of wood to torture the genitalia of the captured Indian.

In 1652, England and the Netherlands were at war, but heavy losses on both sides hurried the prospect of peace. Nevertheless, the two countries' representatives in the New World were increasingly hostile toward each other, even though they were an ocean away from the main belligerents. The Puritans of New England were said to be intent on attacking Manhattan, so preparations were made in New Amsterdam. A wall would be erected at New Amsterdam's northern border, at a cost of 5,000 guilders, with the labor being cheaply supplied by slaves. Made of 15 foot planks, bastions, cannons, and two gates (one at the corner of the present-day intersection of Wall St. and Pearl St., and the other at Wall St. and Broadway).

The Dutch referred to this stretch of road as "de Waal Straat," and it's believed that even before construction of that wall, there were earthen fortifications erected there to protect against Indian attacks. One early history claimed, "The red people from Manhattan Island crossed to the mainland, where a treaty was made with the Dutch, and the place was therefore called the Pipe of Peace, in their language, Hoboken. But soon after that, the Dutch governor, Kieft, sent his men out there one night and massacred the entire population. Few of them escaped, but they spread the story of what had been done, and this did much to antagonize all the remaining tribes against all the white settlers. Shortly after, Nieuw Amsterdam erected a double palisade for defense against its now enraged red neighbors, and this remained for some time the northern limit of the Dutch city. The space between the former walls is now called Wall Street, and its spirit is still that of a bulwark against the people."

The location of the wall would eventually become the center of the financial world, but ultimately, the wall proved as useless as all other Dutch defenses and strategies. In 1664, Colonel Richard Niccolls was sent by the English Duke of York to take Manhattan and all other Dutch holdings. Niccolls sent the Dutch colony's director, Peter Stuyvesant, a letter that promised life and liberty for all if the inhabitants would lay down their arms and surrender. Stuyvesant hid this letter and tore up another, but powerful residents in New Amsterdam forced him to give up in the face of too formidable an enemy. In the end, the diversity of New Amsterdam helped assure that the people would rather become part of New York City than lose everything. The Dutch briefly reclaimed the city, but the tide had turned, and New York became an English settlement. For their own part, the Lenni-Lenape who had lived there for so long dwindled until there were only about 200 of them left at the beginning of the 18th century.

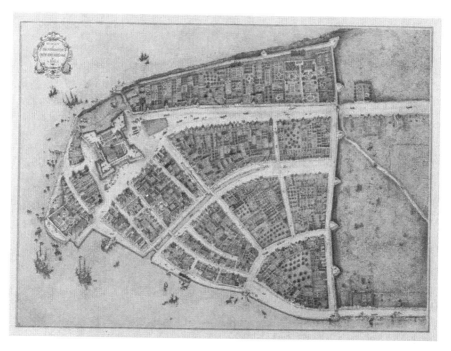

A map of New Amsterdam in 1660 with the wall on the far right of the settlement

Stuyvesant

Just before the end of the 17th century, the remainder of the actual wall on Wall Street was gone, and it would soon become a marketplace, which would make Wall Street a natural place for future exchanges.

Chapter 2: The Birth of European Stock Exchanges

"After a certain point, money is meaningless. It ceases to become the goal. The game is what counts." – Aristotle Onassis, Greek shipping magnate

The idea of investment harks back to Ancient Greece. In a time when much of the world was uncharted and communities scattered around the world relied on ship tradesmen for resources, opportunity dawned. Ship captains reached out to the wealthy to finance their trading voyages, offering investors part of the profits from their loots. With massive but crudely built ships, equipment, and temperamental waters, this was considered one of the earliest practices of investment. Injecting money into these voyages was never a sure thing – the ships could come back with riches, or they were never to be seen again.

Ancient Romans were one of the first to sell stock for construction they could not finance on their own. These early stock brokers raked in plump profits from backing companies that built aqueducts, roads, and other public construction for the government. Across Europe, moneylenders became crucial to sealing the financial holes created by banks. These moneylenders began to barter debts between one another, some of which were government debts. Lenders hoping to relieve themselves of the burden of risky debts with ugly interest rates sought out debts they could handle from other lenders. As the practice went on, moneylenders began selling debt issues to customers. These customers became some of the earliest individual investors.

Come the 1300s, Venice became the forefront of the practice. Traveling merchants began to trade securities from various governments. These merchants were the first stock brokers. They roamed from door to door with slates clutched to their chests, which listed information on the different issues for sale.

In 1531, the world saw its first stock exchange in Antwerp, Belgium. Brokers and moneylenders alike congregated in the Antwerp Bourse, a grand and spacious wooden inn sporting high ceilings and a glass roof. Here, bonds, commodities, and promissory notes were dealt. Government, business, and individual debt issues would also be tackled. Though no actual stocks or shares existed in the 1500s, partnerships between businesses and financiers generated income much like stock does today.

Word of the goings-on in the Antwerp Bourse quickly spread. 40 years later, Queen Elizabeth I established The Royal Exchange in London, England. The architecture of the Antwerp Bourse largely inspired that of The Royal Exchange building.

When the 1600s rolled around, the Dutch, British, and French governments made a move that would pivot the course of economic history. All companies with "East India" in their name were granted charters. The imperialistic move ensured that profits were exclusive to seemingly everyone but the East Indies and Asian natives themselves.

During this time, sea voyages were still largely depended on for trade. Up to this point, investors were still backing one voyage at a time in faltering hopes of partial profits. These were known as the first limited liability companies. When the voyage ended, the company was scrapped, and a new company would be developed. Investors were coughing up currency for a wide range of voyages in one go. Needless to say, those who took the gamble on ships that never returned were faced with debilitating losses.

The merging of the East India companies meant the start of a new chapter. Instead of investing voyage by voyage, companies would have stocks that paid dividends on all voyages a single company undertook. Thus began the world's first joint stock companies.

With this in place, companies could construct larger and more powerful fleets, as well as reel in more profits from their shares. Investors were floating high on Cloud 9. Not only did these charters ban competition, the sheer size of these new companies meant a nifty payday for investors.

Shares were issued on paper, but there was no physical stock exchange for the East India companies. If an investor wanted to sell their share, they would have to employ a broker to carry out the task. Flyers with the latest debt issues and market shares were mailed as newsletters or posted on shop doors for public consumption.

More of the public became intrigued with investment and trade, with many in the middle class trying their hand at the game. But as they would soon learn, the game is a roller coaster of highs and lows, and it runs on unpredictable tracks. In the worst cases, a bubble slowly can slowly froth over an economy. A "bubble" is defined as rapid price increases triggered by a series of irrational market decisions. One inevitable prick could devastate the entire economy of a community.

The earliest record of an economic bubble took place in the Netherlands in 1637 – Tulip Mania. Many have since studied this infamous incident as a 400-year-old cautionary tale, one that Gordon Gekko himself has framed in his office. In the early 1600s, tulips were all the rage in the Netherlands. The Dutch fell smitten with the pretty pastel flowers, and it soon became a must-have in all households, the hottest commodity on the market. The rarity of these seasonal flowers only spurred the demand. People started pressuring the suppliers for reassurance that they would have their beloved tulips by the end of the year. To remedy the demand, suppliers set up a "future's market." In simpler terms, they began taking pre-orders. During the off-season, suppliers sold customers IOUs for tulips, which they could exchange for tulips when they were available.

It wasn't long before suppliers took notice of the unbelievable demand and began jacking up the prices. By 1637, the ludicrously inflated prices took its toll, and the Dutch found themselves in piping-hot water. The price of a perishable bulb was valued at 10 times the yearly salary of a skilled craftsman. To put this into perspective, this meant 10 years of hard labor to get one's hands on a measly flower, only for it to shrivel in 10 days or less. The bubble was eventually popped, and prices plummeted to reasonable levels. Unfortunately, a large number of families were unable to escape from the tulip contracts they had signed at the peak of Tulip Mania, and as a result, lost their family fortunes.

Another significant historical bubble came into play in England, most commonly known as the South Sea Bubble of 1720. The British East India Company was operating on a legal monopoly. This meant an independent company owned all or the majority of a particular market with the government's approval. With little to no competition, investors soon had dollar signs for eyes. Others began wising up to the fortunes being made by investors when they sold their shares, and wanted in. But with the economical boom growing more explosive by the minute, issuing shares was going unregulated. Things quickly got out of hand.

Robert Harley and John Blunt, the founders of the South Sea Company, were also granted a similar charter by King George I. The SSC began passing out countless re-issues of shares like candy, most of which sold as soon as they were listed. Before the first company ship even budged, the SSC used the excessive riches they made from the eager investors to set up state-of-the-art offices in the swankiest parts of the city.

Devious businessmen soon caught on to the SSC's success. Seeing that the SSC had done nothing but sell shares before they even started their first venture, crooked businessmen emerged from the shadows. They approached the public with brand new shares from completely fabricated companies.

Surprisingly, investors were duped by these fictitious ventures and the shady broker's fraudulent claims. In an effort to boost capital and stock prices, these claims became creatively absurd. This included proposals for hair trading and reclaiming sunshine from plants and vegetables. Some invested in wild inventions such as a wheel for perpetual motion and a new-age device that would convert chickens into sheep. One bold company sold shares for a mysterious product so important and shrouded in secrecy, the investors themselves weren't allowed to know what it was. This proved to be a fruitful tactic as the company shares promptly sold out.

Their method of salesmanship was so toxic, a term was coined for it – blind pools. Blind pools are stock offerings with muddy to no investment goals. Investors relied on the name of the individual or company. These risky offerings come with paltry restrictions that are often left unguarded.

Harsh reality struck when the SSC was unable to pay any dividends from their nearly non-existent profits. The crash that ensued crippled the British economy, causing the government to banish the issuing of shares. This ban wouldn't be lifted until 1825.

Soon, the reputations of stock brokers soured. Those on the sidelines agreed that the greedy and dishonest individuals, some of which were disgraced government officials, got what was coming to them. The public disdain for stock brokers soon spread around the globe. It did not help matters when escaped Scottish murderer, John Law, trapped the French public in his blind pools, promising them shares in imaginary gold mines.

Chapter 3: The Exchange Comes to Wall Street

"The terrible, cold, cruel part is Wall Street. Rivers of gold flow there from all over the earth, and death comes with it. There, as nowhere else, you feel a total absence of the spirit: herds of men who cannot count past 3..." – Federico Garcia Lorca, Spanish poet

Wall Street in the 1780s

In 1790, Philadelphia founded the country's first ever stock exchange. The Board of Brokers from the Philadelphia Merchant's Exchange initially held their meetings in the City Tavern. With the blossoming populace of the city, the brokers knew they would soon outgrow the London Coffee House quarters. So, they set out to build their own headquarters from scratch. On the corner joining Second and Walnut Street, wealthy merchants, vessel captains, and other wealthy individuals teamed up to build an opulent 4-story building capped with handsome multiple gable roofs and dozens of rooms.

Finally, the Philadelphia Merchant's Exchange was open for business. A business card from the innkeeper during its opening year described what was to be expected at the new tavern. The 2 large conference rooms in the front of the establishment were open to brokers for use from noon to 2PM, and 6 to 8 in the evening. In the tavern, one could enjoy the stable, newly furnished rooms, and have some grub and drink at the bar, all of which came at "reasonable rates." Later, in 1865, the Board of Brokers rebranded the merchant's exchange as the Philadelphia Stock Exchange.

Back in New York, early stock brokers claimed their territory on Wall Street. The meetings of early brokers transpired in the cool shade of a buttonwood tree. Here, merchants auctioned off stocks from banks and mines, and received commissions of 0.25% from every successful sale. The spirited chatter from hustling merchants in the open-air exchange could be heard throughout the block of 68 Wall Street. Shortly after, they began to conduct their daily meetings at the Tontine Coffee House, which were held twice a day.

A depiction of the buttonwood tree

1797 oil on linen of the Tontine Coffee House, Merchant's Coffee House, and Wall Street, leading down to the East River, by Francis Guy (1760–1820)

In 1789, George Washington was sworn in as the first president at Federal Hall, located along Wall Street, and 3 years later, 24 influential merchants crafted The Buttonwood Agreement. It was a pact promising to bar government intervention from their open-air market, and to shun away all newcomers. The only way outsiders could purchase stock was to go through an approved broker. Following the agreement, the merchants moved to a rented room on 40 Wall Street, effectively excluding themselves from the public eye.

Hearing of the thriving Philadelphia Merchant's Exchange, Wall Street authorities dispatched observers to the state. When the observers returned and relayed the information they learned to their superiors, the New York Stock and Exchange Board came to fruition on March 8, 1817. They later shortened the name to the New York Stock Exchange in 1863. Word traveled through the grapevine, and Wall Street became known as the auction block for slaves.

Along with slave auctions, Wall Street became notorious for enforcing public humiliation. Prisoners, many of which had committed the crime of perjury, had their necks and wrists cuffed by wooden pillories. Mobs of people attended the public humiliations to jeer and hurl rotten vegetables at the shackled prisoners.

In 1817, the NYSE formed their own constitution protecting their exclusivity, and laid a fixed schedule in place. Each morning started off with Anthony Stockholm, president of the board, reciting the stocks available for trade. To obtain a seat in the hush-hush club, one had to be voted in. The potential candidate can also be refused by 3 non-consenting votes. A seat on the exchange cost $25 (approximately $441 USD buying power today). Just a decade later, the price ballooned to $100 ($1,763 USD). By 1848, it was at $400 a pop. The private club even had their own uniforms – a wardrobe of top hats and dark swallowtail coats.

As years passed, the New York Merchant Group realized their stock exchange was failing. This came as a consequence of plunging war bonds and stocks in the Bank of the United States. At this time, only 30 companies held a place in the exchange. These included reputable banks, construction firms, and cargo companies.   Buyers were limited to what historians described as "fearless investors." They were thought of as gamblers, filthy rich, or had intentions of taking over a company. The average individual was terrified of stocks, as the bankruptcy of a company meant stock owners could blow their life savings completely. Uninvited brokers, otherwise known as "curbstone brokers," were left to trade less reputable stocks on the streets, where disagreements often led to a couple of punches or full-out brawls. They later formed their own exchange, dubbing it the American Stock Exchange.

Most importantly, the club's exclusivity was only throttling business. They needed to keep up with the times, as the rest of the world was allowing anyone to join the market. The only advantage from keeping it a private club was that the fixed number of brokers could regulate themselves, thereby avoiding fraud. Begrudgingly, the NYSE opened its doors to the public once more.

Mall Street in 1829

Depiction of Wall Street in 1825 and 1829

When the exchange's rented office at 40 Wall Street was destroyed by a fire that engulfed the entire building in 1835, the board relocated to an office on 10-12 Street. There they stayed until the end of the 19th century, moving when the members outgrew that office, too. By then, with the help of the westward expansion, business at the stock exchange had flourished.

The New York Stock Exchange in the 1880s

Architect George B. Post was assigned to design the new building, the very same that stands today. Construction began in May of 1901. The old buildings from 10-12 Street were scrapped to make way for the new building. During construction, passersby marveled at the looming Corinthian pillars and the brilliant neoclassical facade. The Piccirilli Brothers were in charge of crafting the pediment, with the sculptures featured molded by John Quincy Adams Ward. When it was finished, they christened the pediment "Integrity Protecting the Works of Man." $4 million and 2 years later, construction concluded. On April 22, 1903, the office was officially open.

At 109 x 140 feet, coupled with a ceiling that hovered 72 feet off the ground, the trading floor was one of the largest spaces the 20th century had ever seen. The interior was equally majestic, with the walls and floors covered with sleek marble. The rooms were cooled with the first ever air-conditioning system, an invention that had been introduced to the world just a year before. In the hopes of creating a pleasant atmosphere, brokers were greeted with perfumed air pumped out of the ventilation system. Stock certificates were safely kept in the hundreds of secure vaults underground. The stocks were treated like inventories and sold like every other over-the-counter product.

20th century pictures of the interior

Technology played a critical role in the steady expansion of Wall Street. When Baron Pavel Schilling invented the telegraph in 1832, the world of finance was never the same. Information could now be spread across the country faster than ever before. Samuel Morse brought the invention to the United States, and in 1837, he launched a demonstration office for the telegraph on Wall Street, just a few doors down from the stock exchange. He charged brokers 25 cents apiece for a peek at the new invention. Brokers were giddy with excitement, passing on the word to everyone they knew. Gone were those days when brokers had to physically walk across the trading floor to search for a single deal.

Before long, Wall Street was festooned with telegraph wires weaving down the blocks. The stock exchange welcomed the telegraph with open arms, a fitting new tool for their free-for-all system. By extinguishing the need for other regional markets around the country, New York became the financial capital of the United States.

In 1867, brokers readily embraced the next technological innovation by Edward A. Calahan from The American Telegraph Company – the stock ticker. Stock tickers were bulky machines with a wheel of ticker tape attached to the top. Ticker tapes were narrow paper strips that were threaded through the machine. The ticker printed abbreviated names of companies, along with volume information and stock transaction prices. As the machine printed, it made a rhythmic ticking sound, which was how the machine earned its name.

With every sale, a clerk would roll up a sheet with the details of the transaction and insert it into a pneumatic tube. These tubes sucked up the paper rolls, zipping through the pipe-like system before reaching its destination at the ticker tape room. Typists were then tasked with releasing the information to the rest of the world. With the aid of the stock ticker and telegraph lines, brokers across the country could be updated with up-to-the-minute prices. Best of all, those beyond the doors of the once clandestine exchange could fully understand what was going on.

On July 8, 1889, *The Wall Street Journal* sold its very first issue at a price of 2 cents per paper. Thanks to Charles Dow, Charles Bergstresser, and Edward Jones of Dow Jones & Company, the famed newspaper altered the face of journalism. Many sprung out of their beds to get their hands on the paper, flipping the page to its most important feature. Known as the "Dow-Jones Industrial Average," it was an index of 12 stocks, their performance graphed by the month. The 12 stocks included some of the country's largest corporations including US Rubber, American Sugar, and General Electric.

Dow

As Wall Street slowly took over the world of finance over the years, they soon developed their own slang. The most frequently heard of the lingo are the "Bulls" and the "Bears." Once used as nicknames for speculators, they are now terms for different stock markets. Bear markets are tainted and often associated with negativity, leading to bubbles and other economic declines. They were given the nickname for its historical significance. Ancient bearskin traders were known for selling their products before actually receiving the supply. They crossed their fingers, hoping for a downturn in the market so they could walk away with larger profits. On the contrary, "Bulls" refer to a positive, upward-trending market, where investor confidence is at its highest. Furthermore, stocks with under-performing stocks or assets are referred to as "Dogs."

"Wolves" are ranked on the top of the pyramid. These powerful investors are considered the hotshots of Wall Street. Ferocious wolves are bloodthirsty investors who would stop at nothing to get to the top, sometimes succumbing to criminal means to get their way. In other countries, these investors are known as "Sharks" or "Tigers."

Next, came the "Ostriches." These are wishful thinkers who fail to act during critical changes in the market. Like the animal, Ostriches dig their heads under the sand, ignoring the news as they pray for better days ahead. Ostriches are also known to go MIA when the market gets tough.

Then, there are the "Pigs." Pigs are investors blinded by greed, resorting to unethical strategies for their deals. These investors are not satisfied with 100% returns, and would borrow money for margins to buy more stocks at higher prices for an even larger profit.

Animal terms are also used for choices investors make on the market. "Sheep" are investors with no strategies or clear paths ahead. They rely on financial advice from others like sheep to a shepherd. Because of their inability to think for themselves, they miss out on opportunities other shrewd investors pounce on. Sheep investors are often mauled by the Bulls and Bears of Wall Street. On that note, ineffective investors are also called "Lame Ducks," characterized by their tendency to "waddle" out of the market. Lame Duck businesses are those that go bankrupt or default on their debts.

In later years, more terms were added to the list of Wall Street lingo. Start-up businesses less than 5 years old valued at over a billion dollars with no stock market history are deemed "Unicorns." "Dragons" are similar to "Unicorns," as these businesses generated more than 100% of investments. "Black Swans" are unpredictable events, even with the help of some of the most elaborate investment models. "Stags," or "Flipping," are traders that buy into a company's IPO (initial public offering). Taking advantage of the rising prices on the market, they sell these shares straight away.

Last, but not least, there is the morbidly termed "Dead Cat Bounce." The almost literal term describes the specific market trend exactly, in which there is a temporary spike in stock prices after a devastating fall. As the Oxford English Dictionary puts it, "If you throw a dead cat against a wall at a high rate of speed, it will bounce, but it is still dead."

With all these terms in mind, there is no wonder why so many call Wall Street "The Jungle."

Chapter 4: An Act of Terror

"I saw the explosion, a column of smoke shoot up into the air and then saw people dropping all around me, some of them with their clothing afire." – Charles P. Dougherty, stock exchange messenger

With the brand new facilities and all the technological advances on Wall Street, business was running smoothly. Following World War I, J.P. Morgan and Company made its name on the legendary street as well. This Goliath of a bank became the most influential institution of its kind in the world. A stroll across the street and one would find the US Sub-Treasury and the Assay Office. And just a few buildings down the road, the hectic commotion from the always-full stock exchange spilled out into the streets. All seemed well.

But just 17 years later after the New York Stock Exchange opened its doors, tragedy struck. It was September 16, 1920. Light showers were expected for the day, but the sidewalks were teeming with brokers, clerks, and other members of the lunchtime crowd hurrying for a quick bite to eat. The streets were jammed with automobiles caught in traffic. Alongside them were a chain of messenger boys on bicycles, blowing raspberries as they waited for the snail-paced traffic to move along.

With an air of impatience gripping the annoyed lunchtime crowd, no one bothered to take a second glance at the mysterious vehicle parked out front of the Assay Office. A shabby horse-drawn wagon sat next to the curb. Taking advantage of the oblivious crowd, the driver of the wagon quietly released the horse reins. Then, the faceless driver hopped off the wagon and slithered into the crowd, making a clean escape down the street before vanishing around the corner.

When the hands of the clock touched noon, the bells from Trinity Church rang across Wall Street. But before the final chime sounded at 12:01, the wagon exploded. In one split second, a thunderous roar blasted through the streets. The sudden blast shook the earth, so powerful it derailed a car a full block down. It propelled the doomed car to the 34th floor of the Equitable Building before it came crashing back to the ground.

The wind quickly carried the roaring billows of flame and dense, pitch-black smoke down the streets. Shrapnel, glass, metal, debris, and bloody chunks of human and horse parts rained from the skies. Andrew Dunn, an employee of J.P. Morgan and Co, was a witness who was lucky enough to escape the blast. He recalled, "That was the loudest noise I ever heard in my life. It was enough to knock you out by itself." Even Joseph P. Kennedy, father of President John F. Kennedy, who was present at the bombing, remembered being flung off his feet by the mere force of the blast.

The wreckage and aftermath of the wagon dynamite can only be described as utter pandemonium. Buildings were wholly destroyed, with one of the casualties being the J.P. Morgan building. Those who were close to the detonation were burnt to crisps, adding the nauseating stench of burning flesh and hair to the screaming frenzy. Some lost their lives or were severely injured, crushed by the debris of crumbling buildings.

A picture after the bombing

In order to achieve maximum damage, the perpetrators piled dozens of iron sash weights on top of the bomb. These weights were narrow, flute-like objects that were used to weigh down the sashes on sash windows. One could be as heavy as 30 lbs. When the weights exploded along with the bomb, a great many were sliced up from the jagged pieces of the lethal shrapnel.

All trading at Wall Street immediately screeched to a halt. Over 2,000 New York City policemen and Red Cross nurses flooded the scene to contain the chaos. Hundreds were burned and maimed, some beyond recognition. 30 civilians were killed on the spot, and another 8 would later succumb to their injuries. Until the Oklahoma City bombing that would take place 75 years later, the Wall Street explosion was the deadliest to date.

When the streets were cleared, investigators began the hunt for the bombers. Though they had no leads on who exactly had orchestrated the bombing, they were certain the target was the J.P. Morgan bank. Some believed those responsible were resentful of the alleged profits the bank made off the devastation of the First World War, but the majority of the victims were made up of low-level clerks and stenographers. J.P. Morgan Jr., the believed target, was off vacationing in

Europe at the time of the blast.

J.P. Morgan, Jr.

The *St. Louis Post-Dispatch*, however, claimed it was terrorism. They stated, "The bomb was not directed at any particular person or property. It was directed against a public, anyone who happened to be near or any property in the neighborhood."

A solid clue came a day later. Postal workers discovered flyers stuffed in the Financial District mailboxes. All bore the same message: "Remember, we will not tolerate any longer. Free the political prisoners, or it will be sure death for all of you." It was signed by the "American Anarchist Fighters." Investigators noticed the flyers' uncanny resemblance to those previously circulated on June of 1919. That terrifying year, the group set off a string of bombs in multiple American cities.

The police pinned the crime on the Galleanists. Led by Luigi Galleani, an authoritative speaker and explosives expert, the Galleanists were a dangerous gang of Italian anarchists with a deep-seated hatred for government. Even more incriminating, the Galleanists were infamous for using iron shaft weights for shrapnel in their explosives.

Since then, no other group has come forward to claim responsibility for the Wall Street attack. That said, an interesting facet of the case came with a mentally unsound tennis champion named Edward Fischer. Fischer was heard warning strangers to stay off Wall Street a few days before the attack. Authorities probed further, but were unable to connect him to the case. The Bureau of

Investigation (known as the FBI today) proceeded to spend more than 3 years tracking down the assailants, but ultimately came up short.

To this day, the case remains ice-cold.

Chapter 5: The Catastrophic Crash of 1929

Pictures of crowds gathering on Wall Street during the stock market crash

"The wires to other cities were jammed with frantic orders to sell... Buyers were few, sometimes wholly absent... This was real panic... When the closing bell rang, the great bull market was dead and buried." – Johnathan Norton Leonard, author of *Three Years Down*

After the Allied Powers victory in World War I, the mood shifted across the nation. The economy picked up, with more families willing to splurge on non-necessities. As factories around the country worked double-time to fill the new orders, it was a seemingly win-win situation for everyone who hitched a ride on the bandwagon. More and more households, particularly in the middle and lower class, indulged themselves with goods and services typically reserved for the upper class. When weekends came along, every seat in the new picture theaters was filled. Phonographs, record collections, and cars adorned the living rooms and garages of these households.

By the 1920s, business at the stock exchange was flowing peachily, and it continued to be the talk of the town. The brokers and clerks were among those in peppier spirits. They were not only grateful for the new facilities, they were pleased with the new, more organized system that came with it.

Each stock was now traded at assigned spots known as posts. Every post served stocks of a different nature, with railroad stocks found in one post and steel stocks in another. This made it easier for brokers to navigate the trading floor. Specialists, sometimes known as Auctioneers, were in charge of the bidding.

The soaring economy lifted the hopes of both Wall Street and the general public alike, continuing to do so over the 1920s. Harold Geneen, who was 16 when he started as a page on the trading floor back in 1926, spoke of his first impression on the stock exchange. He reminisced, "It was a very exuberant period. I thought it was kinda lively and a lot of fun."

The 1920s also opened Wall Street's doors to women. This was revolutionary, unheard of in the once all-boys club. Prior to this, gender prejudice was the only barrier that kept the women outside the Wall Street buildings. Women were thought to be incapable of rational decision-making on the scorching hot trading floor, and lacked the astute foresight men possessed for speculating in the market. But around the country, women were slowly making a stand for themselves. They began cropping up at colleges and unorthodox workplaces, and were now allowed to handle their own finances. Understandably, independent women began setting their eyes on Wall Street, looking to make riches of their own. With every passing year, the number of female Wall Street clerks swelled.

Along with the millions of household goods and the influx of cars sold across the country, the public themselves began to dip their toes in the murky pool of stock and investment. More curious Average Joes turned to the Wall Street Journal to analyze the stocks. They, too, started to purchase shares of their favorite companies, mostly those that made the goodies and cars they owned.

Even celebrities of the era were dabbling in stock investments. The public scoped out the investment activities of actors like celebrated silent-film star, Charlie Chaplin, and famous eyebrow-and-mustache combo, Julius "Groucho" Marx. Many began modeling their own investments after what Chaplin and Marx happened to be speculating on.

Marx was known for dumping all his savings into stock investments. After filming each scene, he would make a beeline for the phone, calling up his broker for updates. He was so delighted with the results, he convinced his brothers to do the same. Later, he shared his triumphs with the public, announcing on the papers, "What an easy racket. [Stock] went up 7 points since this morning. I just made myself $7,000!"

Sentiments like these encouraged the directionless public, but this was not Wall Street's first attempt to hone in on the untapped market. To spice up sales of war bonds during World War I, awareness events were hosted outside Wall Street buildings. Like charity concerts today, they featured a wide range of celebrities, predominantly stars from motion picture films. Alongside Chaplin, America's sweetheart, Martha Mansfield, and lovable tough guy, Douglas Fairbanks, addressed the crowd with conical megaphones. They riled up the public with patriotic speeches which were met with approving hoots and hollers. A gripping headline splashed across the 1918 issue of the New York Tribune read, "20,000 Throng Wall Street to Hear Movie Stars Tell How to Win War." Before these events, the public had no experience on purchasing stocks or bonds. They had no idea what they were getting themselves into.

With the rampant demand for stocks, prices skyrocketed. Between the years of 1924 and 1929, the Dow-Jones Industrial Average rose a whopping 300%. Unbeknownst to the vast majority of the public, a lava of turmoil was bubbling underneath them, and the ground was starting to crack. As Geneen said, "You had a lot of people in the market who knew nothing about the market, except they were going to make some quick money. And the thing was obviously overblown."

Gradually, a new wave of Wall Street Pigs squeezed out of their pens, infiltrating the market. These unsavory brokers pressured their investors to buy dubious stocks. Sheep investors gladly opened both ears to these investors. They fell for thinly veiled lies about how these fabricated companies were about to make it big.

Many investors began to purchase stocks on credit, which was a big no-no in the industry. In Wall Street, this was known as "buying on margin." If the investor was considered a good customer, they were allowed to buy stocks at a 10% margin. To paint a clearer picture, this meant that by putting up just $100, an investor could own a share of a stock valued at $1,000. The remaining $900 credit would then become collateral for a loan. As the public grew increasingly comfortable with purchasing on credit, a few skeptical investors voiced their concerns. They spotted shadows of a storm brewing overhead, wondering how long these "good times" would last.

Among the skeptics were Joseph Kennedy and the once eager advocate, Groucho Marx. Kennedy sensed that something was not sitting right with the market. He wrote in his memoir, "If the shoe shine guy knows as much as I do about the stock market, maybe it's time for me to get out." Marx apparently contacted his broker at one point, complaining that he could not understand why prices kept going up. As a reply, the broker informed him that this was now a "global economy," and things were different, a phrase that has been uttered time and time again. Even Herbert Hoover, the President himself, began to approach his Wall Street friends, wondering if this was cause for alarm.

In 1928, Charles E. Merrill, one of the founders of the Merrill Lynch Firm, issued a daunting warning to his clients. In the letter, Merrill wrote, "Now is a good time to get out of debt. We do not urge that you sell securities indiscriminately, but we do advise, in no uncertain terms, that you should take advantage of present high prices and put your own financial house in order." It appeared that the skeptics' concerns had more validity than they thought.

In 1929, things began to get ugly. The once booming sales of "big ticket" goods tumbled, triggering the decline of multiple big-name stocks. The abrupt decline in the market prompted a nationwide margin call. The phones of investors rang off the hook with thousands of brokers on the other end of the line. Anxious brokers pestered the investors to inject more money into their stock market accounts.

People began to realize the dangers of buying stock on credit. But by then, it was too late. When the price of a stock shrinks, the dwindling worth of the stock is no longer fit to be collateral for the loan. The only way to even out the stock and loan was to push the investors to put up more margins, or scrounge up whatever cash they could give. If investors failed to do so, their accounts were liquidated.

On September 5, Roger Babson told a meeting of the National Business Conference, "I repeat what I said at this time last year and the year before, that sooner or later a crash is coming which will take in the leading stocks and cause a decline of from 60 to 80 points in the Dow-Jones Barometer. Fair weather cannot always continue. The economic cycle is in progress today as it was in the past. The Federal Reserve System has put the banks in a strong position, but it has not changed human nature. More people are borrowing and speculating today than ever in our history. Sooner or later a crash is coming and it may be terrific. Wise are those investors who now get out of debt and reef their sails. This does not mean selling all you have, but it does mean paying up your loans and avoiding margin speculation…Sooner or later the stock market boom will collapse like the Florida boom. Someday the time is coming when the market will begin to slide off, sellers will exceed buyers, and paper profits will being to disappear. Then there will immediately be a stampede to save what paper profits then exist."

Babson

Some people listened to his words and considered them more reliable than those of Evangeline Adams (who was still predicting a rise), and the market dipped in response. This was later called the Babson Break, named after Babson, and two days later, the *Chicago Tribune* reported, "Roger Babson's dire predictions of an 'inevitable crash' in the stock market, which would some time break the averages 60 to 80 points, evoked retorts today from economists, stock exchange houses, and others, most of whom took an opposite view or advised clients and the public not to be stampeded by Mr. Babson's forecast of a collapse that would rival that of the Florida land boom. Mr. Babson's view was directly controverted by Prof. Irving Fisher of Yale University, an economist of highest standing. Prof. Fisher flatly asserted that 'stock prices are not high and Wall Street will not experience anything in the nature of a crash.'"

Over the next few weeks, prices continued to go up and down. Reuban Cain, a stock salesman at the time, later recalled, "I remember well that I thought, 'Why is this doing this?' And then I thought, 'Well, I'm new here and these people' — like every day in the paper, Charlie Mitchell would have something to say, the J.P. Morgan people would have something to say about how good things were — and I thought, 'Well, they know a lot more about this market than I do. I'm fairly new here and I really can't see why it's going up.' But then, when they say it can't go down or if it does go down today, it'll go back tomorrow, you think, 'Well, they really are like God. They know it all and it must be the way it's going because they say so.'"

Meanwhile, *The World* ran a headline on October 4 that read "Brokers to Open Offices on Ships," and the article announced, "The New York Stock Exchange decided yesterday to put to sea. It gave two brokerage houses permission to establish offices with continuous stock quotations by radio, on trans-Atlantic ships. Within a few weeks business will be following the flags of three nations across the bounding main. The American business man will be able to take a vacation in Europe without stopping for a single day his transactions at the center of speculation… What the psychological effect may be remains to be seen. Lady Luck always has been a favorite companion for diversions seekers at sea, a fact that has provided good incomes to many generations of traveling card players. Ships' pools and the 'horse races' on deck always have been popular. They may retain their popularity, but now they will be outclassed."

A few days later, Thomas Lamont, then the head of Morgan Bank, wrote to President Hoover and assured him, "The future appears brilliant. Our securities are the most desirable in the world." As Craig Mitchell later noted, "Practically every business leader in America, and banker, right around the time of 1929, was saying how wonderful things were and the economy had only one way to go and that was up."

On October 24, Wall Street collapsed. The financial pools of thousands of dazed investors were now bone-dry. None of them could hand over the required funds when it was time for their brokers to enter the exchange. At 10 AM sharp, the brass alarm reverberated across the gloomy trading floor, signaling the start of the liquidation sales. Geneen, who was also present on that fateful day, said it was just like any other busy day. But as the day went on, things only got worse. It became clear that no one was interested in buying – everyone was looking to shake off their now questionable stocks.

The usual hubbub on the trading floor morphed into panic. The holes the countrywide "credit binge" were poking had gotten so out of hand, the market quickly collapsed on itself. Stock prices continued to plummet throughout the day, which led to even more margin calls that resulted in liquidation. Desperate brokers were selling so many shares at once that the ticker was lagging on a 4-hour delay. Worried investors clogged the streets outside the entrance, demanding to know what was going on.

Out of nowhere, the Vice President of the exchange, Richard Whitney, took a brave step forward. He summoned the nation's top bankers and trotted off to the trading floor. With a puffed out chest, he purchased $20 million worth of stock, all in a matter of minutes. The public cheered, believing Whitney was here to haul them out of the slump.

Craig Mitchell described the day: "The market opened in an absolutely free fall and some people couldn't even get any bids for their shares and it was wild panic. And an ugly crowd gathered outside the stock exchange and it was described as making weird and threatening noises. It was, indeed, one of the worst days that had ever been seen down there."

Hopeful that he could do something like Charles Mitchell had done back in March, the men of Wall Street turned their eyes to Thomas Lamont, who they hoped would intervene. According to Lamont's grandson Edward, "Tom Lamont called a number of the other bankers, like Charles Mitchell of the National City Bank and people from the Bankers Trust and J. Albert Wiggin of the Chase Bank and so forth — there were about a half a dozen of them there — and they were gathered together to really discuss what they could do to stem this tremendous onslaught of selling stocks on the stock exchange that was taking place."

Charles Mitchell agreed to help. As his son later put it, "About 12:30, there was an announcement that this group of bankers would make available a very substantial sum to ease the credit stringency and support the market. And right after that, Dick Whitney made his famous walk across the floor of the New York Stock Exchange." Arriving at the Stock Exchange, Whitney made a very public showing of ordering 10,000 shares of U.S. Steel at a higher price than it was selling at that time. Horace Silverstone, who was there that day, explained, "He stood up on one of the seats at the post and he said, 'I give 45 for 50,000 Standard Oil,' and everybody started to applaud. 'Oh, the crash is over. If Morgan's putting his money in, then maybe the crash is over.'" Edward Lamont noted that his ancestor felt the same way: "The *New York Times* said that thanks to the formation of this bankers pool, most observers felt that the panic and the great sell-off was over. And most people did feel that way. Tom Lamont felt that way."

Nonetheless, on that Thursday, a *New York Times* headline read "Prices of Stocks Drop in Heavy Liquidation; Total Drop of Billions." According to the report, "Frightened by the decline in stock prices during the last month and a half, thousands of stockholders dumped their shares on the market yesterday afternoon in such an avalanche of selling as to bring about one of the widest declines in history. Even the best of seasoned, dividend paying shares were sold regardless of the prices they would bring, and the result was a tremendous smash in which stocks lost from a few points to as much as ninety-six."

As the next few days passed, the public grew uneasy. It seemed that they had celebrated too early, as Whitney's generosity had nothing to do with saving the market. In fact, he was looking to fool the market so banks could eventually be sold at a higher price.

Nonetheless, on Monday, margin calls compelled investors to sell off their holdings, and the Dow suffered a record loss of over 38 points, representing more than 13% overall. Galbraith explained the events of the day: "Monday, October 28, was the first day on which this process of climax and anticlimax ad infinitum began to reveal itself. It was another terrible day. Volume was huge, although below the previous Thursday— nine and a quarter million shares as compared with nearly thirteen. But the losses were far more severe. The Times industrials were down 49 points for the day. General Electric was off 48; Westinghouse, 34; Tel and Tel, 34. Steel went down 18 points. Indeed, the decline on this one day was greater than that of all the preceding week of panic. Once again a late ticker left everyone in ignorance of what was happening, save that it was bad. On this day there was no recovery. At one-ten Charles E. Mitchell was observed going into Morgan's, and the news ticker carried the magic word. Steel rallied and went from 194 to 198. But Richard Whitney did not materialize. It seems probable in light of later knowledge that Mitchell was on the way to float a personal loan. The market weakened again, and in the last hour a phenomenal three million shares— a big day's business before and ever since— changed hands at rapidly falling prices."

Reporter Jonathan Leonard described the scene in the wake of October 28: "That night Wall Street was lit up like a Christmas tree. Restaurants, barber shops, and speakeasies were open and doing a roaring business. Messenger boys and runners raced through the streets whooping and singing at the tops of their lungs. Slum children invaded the district to play with balls of ticker tape. Well-dressed gentlemen fell asleep in lunch counters. All the downtown hotels, rooming houses, even flophouses were full of financial employees who usually slept in the Bronx. It was probably Wall Street's worst night. Not only had the day been bad, but everybody down to the youngest office boy had a pretty good idea of what was going to happen tomorrow."

It would be known as "Black Monday," but the trouble was far from over. Tuesday, October 29, dawned cold and dreary in New York as the stock market opened to what soon became a disaster. As the day continued, it was clear that panicked investors were doing everything they could to pull out of the market, and by the end of the day, the Dow had lost another 12% of its value overall.

At 9:20 a.m. that morning, Lawrence Richey, President Hoover's secretary, telegraphed him: "Mr. President: – Mr. Rand, of Remington-Rand Company New York has just telephoned stating that he thinks you should issue statement to the press tonight for publication tomorrow morning, such as this:— 'I am of the opinion that speculators excessives have been thoroughly liquidated [sold] and sound investment securities [stocks and bonds] have been reduced to a safe and attractive [price] level. Now is the time for Bankers, Brokers, and Investors to exercise the utmost of patience and cool judgment in all dealings with one another.' Mr. Rand states that conditions are very serious and if exist for day or two longer as they have for past few days, will result in ruining millions of business people. States reaction not alone in New York, but all over the Country, as he has been in touch with different sections of the country over long-distance phone, and states business people of the Country are looking to you for some such statement to save the situation."

The World's optimistic headline read "Gigantic Bank Pool Pledged To Avert Disaster as Second Big Crash Stuns Wall Street Largest Financial Powers in the City Meet After Day of Hysterical Liquidation Sinking Prices Below Thursday's." The article reported, "After the stock market had come crashing down again in a veritable deluge of forced and hysterical liquidation, word sped through the financial district last evening that the largest banks in the city were prepared to exert their organized power this morning to prevent further disaster. Arrangements described as "fully adequate" were completed at a conference at the offices of J. P. Morgan & Co. at Broad and Wall Streets… Although no formal statement was issued, it was the consensus of those at the meeting that the worst of the liquidation is over and that a natural demand for investment stocks now available on the bargain counter should go far toward an immediate restoration of trading stability."

Obviously that did not work, and the next day the *New York Evening Post* reported, "It is clear that the Street is going through the greatest disaster in its history. No fair words can gloss over that fact. Because there is no tightness of money we are without the most familiar feature of a bad [economic] time. Furthermore, the stock market has been operating so independently of business that we have not yet realized the larger results of its break. Nevertheless, good must come even from this stern and cruel housecleaning. The country will go back to work…That means here, as it meant in postwar Germany, a revival of values. How can any cool head fail to agree with Professor Irving Fisher's declaration that standard American stocks have gone so much too low as to be crying to be bought? Such stocks are the bone and sinew of the country. Not to believe in them is not to believe in America. The world has so many things that must be done, and no one can do them better than our own people. Our business strength has pulled us out of difficulties in days gone by. With faith it will do it again."

By the end of the week, General Electric, which was once valued at $1,612 per share, dropped to $154. Automobile giant General Motors went from $1,075 each to a measly $40. The Dow-Jones Industrial Average shot down 89%. Perhaps the most sobering statistic of all, over $72 billion of investments were flushed down the drain. Those that had bet their entire life savings on these investments were beside themselves, seeing countless families ruined.

Groucho Marx was unable to escape the wrath of the depression. He was said to have been emotionally traumatized by the crash, slipping into a "lifelong struggle with insomnia." Still, despite the loss of his life savings, Marx was considered one of the lucky ones. He was in a profession that allowed him to continue to earn a living throughout the years of the depression. Arthur Marx recalled, "My father was ready to kill himself. In the morning of the crash, he got a call and it was Max Gordon and Max Gordon says, 'Groucho?' and my father said, 'What?' And Gordon said, 'Groucho, the jig is up.'"

Reuben Cain, who had been a stock salesman up until the time of the crash, said, 'There were all sorts of rumors and you'd see people going down the street looking up to see if they could catch somebody jumping out the window. Now, it turned out there weren't as many people who jumped out the window as they reported, but some did and others committed suicide other ways."

Rita Cushman later remembered, "This house was taken over, of course, and things changed. And I began to know what the real world was all about. It was about time. I was 19 years old." Her father ended October 1929 with $12 million in debt but paid off what he owed and lived long enough to die in 1955 as a respected member of Wall Street.

One historian described the instantaneous effects it had elsewhere: "Five hundred miles from Wall Street in the Atlantic, the luxury liner, the Berengaria, was heading home. From Michael Meehan's brokerage office, word spread through the ship: 'The bottom's fallen out of the market.' Men came running out of their Turkish baths in towels. Card games ended abruptly. Everyone tried to jam into the tiny office, yelling, 'Sell at market!' They had left England wealthy men. They docked in New York without a penny."

On a side note, one of the most interesting myths about Wall Street is tied to this crash. As the myth goes, ruined brokers were throwing themselves out of windows in droves. Allegedly, clerks in hotels were asking customers whether they wanted a room for sleeping or jumping upon checking in. The reality was this was merely an example of the media spinning stories out of control. After the 1929 crash, there were over 100 documented suicides, and only 4 were linked to the crash. However, it appeared more people resorted to self-immolation, self-inflicted gunshots, gassing, and jumping from bridges as suicide methods.

This downward spiral carried on for the following 3 years. For a full decade, the United States felt the burn of one what experts call the "worst economic collapse in the history of the modern industrial world." While the public sunk deeper into the Great Depression, they grew hostile towards Wall Street. They blamed the smooth-talking members of Wall Street for causing the crash.

There was no doubt about it – something had to be done.

Chapter 6: A Time for Change

"After the collapse of Wall Street in the 1920s, the culture stopped being all about the money, and the country survived and ultimately flourished." – Graydon Carter, *Vanity Fair* editor

In 1932, the United States welcomed Franklin Roosevelt as the country's 32nd president, and his very first speech to the public was a firm message that called for immediate change. He targeted the stock market as his first call for reform. Standing behind a podium before thousands of spectators, he announced, "There must be strict supervision of all banking, and credit, and investment. There must be an end to speculation of other people's money." With every breath between each proclamation, the crowd received him with raucous applause.

When President Roosevelt stepped into office in 1933, he went to work immediately. On the second day of his presidency, he ordered the New York stock exchange offices to close for a week. Then, he tackled Congress, ticking off a list of reforms that were to be put into action as soon as possible.

First, banks were no longer allowed to "gamble" on stocks. The tarnished reputation of stock brokers was to end right then. Brokers were now expected to treat their customers' money as if it were their own. If corporations wished to resume offering stocks to the public, they had to file detailed financial reports with a government agency every year. With the ability to gain access to clearer information, as well as the tighter and more regulated system set in place, the public's confidence in stock investment was restored.

At this stage, Richard Whitney had been promoted to President of the stock exchange. As to be expected, he was less than pleased with President Roosevelt's sweeping reforms. He appeared on live television, speaking ill of the new regulations and stating that Wall Street was fully equipped to handle matters on their own. In plainer terms, he wanted the government to stay out of Wall Street.

In spite of Whitney's televised threats, President Roosevelt was not fazed. It only fired up his drive for government control over Whitney's precious Wall Street. On June 6, 1934, he founded the Securities and Exchange Commission (SEC) with the sole task of enforcing these rules. Joseph Kennedy was assigned as the SEC's first chairman.

The SEC indicted an alarming number of over 300 people. The Pigs and Wolves of Wall Street either retreated into the shadows or were forced to change their ways, hoping to evade the patrolling eyes of the SEC. Even with the indictments, the SEC had trouble making any of the convictions stick, but many felt deep satisfaction when the only major figure to ever be convicted was none other than Whitney. He was charged with embezzlement and carted off to the notorious Sing Sing Prison, where he spent a total of 3 years.

Regardless of President Roosevelt's new regulations, the Wall Street craze fizzled. The people lost their ravenous hunger for paper exchange, and brokers quit in droves, leaving in search for concrete jobs with a steadier paycheck.

Unlike the First World War, the federal government funded the effort to jumpstart the economy after World War II. The stock market was only responsible for 20%. Though Wall Street had seen better years financially, the end of the war in September of 1945 gifted them with a positive turning point.

Before this, women were only allowed in the back rooms of the Wall Street offices. They were limited to jobs with lighter responsibilities such as clerks and stenographers. In 1945, the first batch of female stock brokers joined the men on the trading floor. Dressed in classy collared dresses fitted with shoulder pads, the women marched onto the floor, ready to make a name for themselves.

The years that followed the war were prosperous, running on the nation's refreshed ambition – the Baby Boom years. Once again, the public warmed up to the idea of stock investment. Investors learned from the mistakes of those that had lost everything in the 1929 crash. They were now wiser, making calculated decisions as opposed to speculating.

Charles Merrill took advantage of the steadily growing economy and seized his opportunity. He opened up hundreds of new Merrill Lynch offices in the suburbs. This was an insightful move on his part, tweaking the damaged reputation of Wall Street stock brokers. Next, Merrill put out several ads on the papers, listing the qualities of his ideal candidates. The ad read, "The person we're after is a GI, ex-GI, with a wife, 3 kids, and a Chevy." It appeared as if an average, middle class citizen had a real shot at making it big in the business someday.

The women of the community were not forgotten. Merrill set up a series of investment classes for women, all of which he personally taught. An empty seat in these classes was a rarity. Later, Merrill erected a pop-up "How to Invest" exhibit in New York's Grand Central Station. The exhibit featured multiple television screens propped up on all 4 sides, along with Merrill Lynch employees beyond tables handing out information pamphlets and research booklets for free.

Another significant innovation that would take Wall Street and the public by storm came with economist Harry Markowitz from the University of Chicago. In 1952, he published an essay focusing on what he called the "Modern Portfolio Theory." In the industry, it is better known as "stock diversification." Markowitz encouraged investors all over the country to purchase a wide range of stocks from different fields. This, he believed, would boost one's chances against bankruptcy if one stock were to fail. Eventually, this radical idea earned Markowitz a Nobel Prize for Economics, and today, many investors still play by Markowitz's golden rule.

Chapter 7: The Age of Computers

"Technology...is a queer thing. It brings you great gifts with one hand, and it stabs you in the back with the other." – C.P. Snow

As the United States transitioned to the 1960s and 1970s, the market saw its fair share of bad days. Yet another disaster was about to strike, but this was one that was unlike any other. Wall Street had unwillingly entered what many refer to today as the 1960s Paperwork Panic.

There were now more brokers on the trading floor than ever. Plus, with the rising figures of mutual funds and pension plans, trading volume was now at a staggering 11 million shares a day.

The problem was, these 11 million trades were implemented by hand. Clerks clocked out each day with a strained back and gelatin legs from being hunched over and on their feet all day. Most were suffering from paper cuts and cases of "trigger finger," kneading their misshapen fingers caused by hours of vigorous scribbling. During working hours, mountains of stacked papers were a common sight on the clerks' desks. Naturally, the increasing volume of paperwork led to delays. Every week, barely lucid clerks were unable to finish their paperwork in time. The problem became so dire that the stock exchange at New York began closing their doors on Wednesdays so the clerks could catch up on their work. Cots started to pop up all over the offices. Clerks were so exhausted from working around the clock that they worked out shifts. While the others worked, 1 or 2 were allowed to duck out of the room for a quick snooze on the cots. With some of the worst cases, clerks would not leave the office for weeks.

The clerks' exhaustion was one matter, but many began to abuse the delirium on the trading floor from the endless paper-crunching. There were common mix-ups from communication errors. These prompted failed trades, brokerages, and market shutdowns.   And then there were those that took the chance to milk the system. A *New York Times* article that researched Wall Street's activities from 1967-1970 reported that there were over $400 million in stolen securities. Today, that is a figure equivalent to $2.8 billion. The same article reported that one 22-year-old broker was charged with stealing over $900,000 in IBM stock certificates.

Perhaps the gravest setback of all was the cash flow chaos that ensued. The crisis was at its height in 1968. In a few months' time, nearly 100 companies filed for bankruptcy.

In addition to the complications from the Vietnam War, politically charged issues from the Kennedy to Carter years contributed to market upsets. One of these major events was the OPEC Oil Crisis of 1973. The members of the Organization of Arab Petroleum Exporting Companies ceased oil trade with Japan, Canada, the Netherlands, the United Kingdom, and the United States. A year after the ban, the price per barrel had shot up from $3 to $12 in the United States. Gas stations across the country were at their wit's end, scrambling to service the long lines of troubled Americans waiting for a gallon of gas.

Wall Street stumbled upon its saving grace with yet another striking technological advance – computers. In the 1970s, Wall Street replaced their antiquated ticker machines and paper-pushing system with its first electronic system. Now, smaller transactions were sent straight to their assigned trading posts. Clerks were finally relieved of the draining handwritten task, and computers were now programmed to handle the quickly swelling volume of trades.

The National Association of Securities Dealers Automated Quotations, or NASDAQ, was founded by the NASD in 1971. In February of 1971, they began trading as the world's first ever electronic stock market. Stock trading was now based on a computerized bulletin board system, as well as over the phone. NASDAQ provided an inexpensive way to trade, cutting corners to render face-to-face encounters obsolete. Brokerage houses were now linked around the globe.

By the 1980s, Wall Street had become completely reliant on the new computerized system, and little did anyone know, this exact entity was about to betray them. On October 19, 1987, Wall Street was hit with another wave of déjà vu. The market was failing – and fast.

Computers were still running on what many today consider an archaic system. They were pre-programmed to automatically sell stocks when prices reached a certain number. One simple press of a button and the stock was sold. This created a chain reaction, setting off one computer after another. With trading volumes higher than ever, it was a fiasco even all the clerks in Wall Street put together could not contain. The Dow-Jones Average sunk 508 points, losing 22.6% of its value. This translated to a ground-quaking loss of over $500 billion. October 19th of 1987 is now glumly remembered as "Black Monday," one of the largest one-day crashes in all of Wall Street history.

Black Monday was a brutal day for Wall Street, but like other disasters, experts learned from it. The NYSE revamped the computers with a circuit-breaker program. This program fixed the bug, restricting trading in the case of unsteady DOW fluctuations.

Chapter 8: The 2008 Housing Fiasco

"Many of us like to think of financial economics as a science, but complex events like the financial crisis suggest that this conceit may be more wishful thinking than reality." – Andrew Lo, MIT professor

On December 15, 1989, enthusiastic crowds on Broad Street assembled outside the NYSE building. A 7,000 lb sculpture of a handsome bull was sitting under a towering Christmas tree. Earlier that morning, Sicilian artist Arturo DiModica snuck onto Broad Street with his masterpiece. Having timed the schedule of the roaming security, he dropped the bull off under the tree and went on his merry way. This was DiModica's gift to the American public. Standing at 11 feet, with an imposing 18 foot long torso, the "Charging Bull" symbolized "the power of the American people." Intentionally installed just 2 years after Black Monday, DiModica wanted to reinvigorate the people's spirit, bringing light to their unyielding determination and the better days coming ahead.

Since no one had ordered the statue, Wall Street authorities got rid of it the same day. The move made the *New York Post* headlines the next morning: "Bah, Humbug! New York Stock Exchange Grinches Can't Bear Christmas Gift Bull." The City of New York graciously accepted the gift instead, and the "Charging Bull," a.k.a the "Wall Street Bull," is now permanently residing in Bowling Green Park.

The decades that followed saw a few hiccups in the market, but all in all, Wall Street sailed to the 2000s. During 9/11, Wall Street suffered some of the damage, including physically. The *New York Times* reported, "Debris littered some streets of the financial district. National Guard members in camouflage uniforms manned checkpoints. Abandoned coffee carts, glazed with dust from the collapse of the World Trade Center, lay on their sides across sidewalks. Most subway stations were closed, most lights were still off, most telephones did not work, and only a handful of people walked in the narrow canyons of Wall Street yesterday morning." It was estimated that a substantial portion of Wall Street's office space was hopelessly ruined.

In 2008, Wall Street witnessed a catastrophe that would not only affect the United States but billions around the world. On September 29, 2008, the Dow-Jones Average took a hurtling nosedive of 777.68 points. The ghastly crash came after Congressmen rejected a $700 billion bailout bill.

How did it come to this? The start of 2007 seemed to be a promising year. The Dow-Jones Average was closing at a glowing figure of approximately 12,460. Coming a long way from its early years, the Average had grown from observing 12 to the 30 most significant stocks trading on the NYSE and NASDAQ. As months passed, the Average continued to scale new heights. October 2007 saw the Average at an all-time high: 14,164.43.

Still, some were disturbed by the climbing Average. Chin-stroking skeptics, who had noticed the slowdown of the turbulent housing market, began to raise red flags. Some of these skeptics had already begun to smell fish the year prior. The most memorable of these red flags was the warning issued by The Commerce Department in November of 2006. For the month of October, the number of new home permits was 28% lower than it had been in October of 2005. The housing market suffered a huge plunge in prices in 2006, inevitably leading to defaults on sub-prime mortgages.

The mortgage was a phenomenon invented by insurance companies in the 1930s. To buy a house, many families turned to these insurance companies for substantial loans. In exchange, they received a piece of paper called a "mortgage." Every month, homeowners were expected to pay back portions of the loan attached with interest rates. Failed payments granted these insurance companies or banks the right to confiscate the homeowner's properties.

Authorities soon realized that the mortgage payment system was detrimental to the average family. Over a period of 3-5 years, mortgage loan terms were limited to 50% of the house's market value, and the payment ended with a balloon sum. In 1934, the Federal Housing Administration established the modern mortgage still used today, enforcing new regulations with banks across the nation. A new, stricter program was aimed at those who were not eligible for the previous programs.

Today, mortgages operate in a similar fashion. If a homeowner was to stop paying their mortgage, they would have to default. The mortgage is often passed on from one bank or company to another. Those with their hands on the mortgage are then granted ownership of the house. It is very common for banks to sell mortgages to third parties.

Back then, banks were only interested in candidates that could give proof of steady income and above-average credit, but in the 2000s, this attitude began to change. The market saw an alarming increase of sub-prime mortgages, which were loans given to potential homeowners with poor credit ratings who did not qualify for traditional mortgages. To level out the risk, the bank or company slapped on a higher interest rate.

For the first years of the new millennium, investors began pouring their money into the housing market. By doing so, the investors hoped to plump up their cash cows with profits from the interest rates that homeowners paid on their mortgages. Once trusted bonds like the U.S. Treasury were now losing its luster, paying what the investors considered to be scant interest rates, so fat-cat global investors began purchasing mortgage-backed securities. This is when financial institutions "securitize" mortgages. Securitizing is when assets that are not easily converted to cash are turned into securities. The investors indulged themselves with a shopping spree of thousands of individual mortgages. They then balled up these mortgages in one pool and sold shares of it to other investors. Across the country, thousands of investors competed for a dip in that pool.

From the exterior, these shares seemed like perfectly safe bets. After all, the housing market was apparently on the rise. Investors believed that if worst came to worst and borrowers defaulted on their mortgages, the house would simply be sold for more money. Even credit ratings agencies promoted the idea of mortgage-backed securities to their customers as secure investments. These agencies went so far as to award the securities with "AAA" ratings.

Investors were desperate to quench their now intensifying thirst for mortgage-backed securities. Lenders needed to figure out a way to fulfill that demand. To do so, they needed more mortgages, so banks and companies across the nations lowered their standards, granting more sub-prime mortgages than they ever had. They targeted humble households with poor credit ratings and low income. This was already a practice that was frowned upon in the industry, but slippery institutions started getting greedy.

These institutions began utilizing tactics called "predatory lending practices" to create mortgages. They passed out loans carelessly without conducting background checks or verifying income. The adjustable rate mortgages offered by these companies were tricky and unfairly sugarcoated. These were payments people could afford initially, but would grow beyond their means in no time.

Sub-prime mortgages and newfangled predatory lending practices were still unknown to the majority of the public, and these companies wanted to keep it that way. This gave them the freedom to promote mortgage debts as stellar bets. The reality was the exact opposite, but the investors' faith in ratings was solid, and they continued to fatten up this new segment of the market with their dough. An even riskier product that traders began to offer were CDOs – collateralized debt obligations.

At the same time, the increasingly lax lending requirements, along with sinking interest rates, drove up housing prices. This gave the public more reason to believe these were wise investments. As the skeptics predicted, the nation found themselves in yet another bubble.

The bubble burst. People failed to keep up with their constantly growing mortgage payments. Like dominoes, the borrowers began defaulting, giving them no choice but to put up more houses for sale. Unfortunately, buyers now had cold feet – no one was looking to buy.

Next, home prices went from fumbling to a lightning-fast tumble. Some families were now lugging around hulking mortgages way more than their homes were actually worth. Then, those borrowers who could not make the monthly bills were forced to default too, pushing housing prices down even further.

Huge financial institutions that were once on the up and up ceased all purchase of sub-prime mortgages. Sub-prime lenders were now piling up on shoddy loans. By 2007, some of the biggest lenders in the business filed for bankruptcy. The investment from investors who had injected big money into these CDOs and mortgage-backed companies virtually evaporated.

Fanning the flames was another dilemma many of these financial institutions had overlooked. Banks had been selling unregulated derivatives on the market, the most serious of which were credit default swaps. Swaps were exchanged as insurance policies for mortgage-backed securities. One of the major companies that fell prey to this was the American International Group (AIG). AIG sold billions of dollars worth of these policies without having sufficient funds to back them up in the event of an emergency.

All these problems only added to a convoluted tangle of assets, liabilities, and risks. Everything was connected, so when things went wrong, it impacted the entirety of the complex entity.

The unsettled public watched as some of the country's major companies fell into decline. The Lehman Brothers declared bankruptcy. Others followed suit, were forced to enter mergers, or had to knock on the government's door for bailouts.

As a result, in September 2008, everything came undone. Wall Street and credit markets were at a standstill, unleashing another storm of nationwide panic. That year, the United States faced another one of its worst recessions.

2008 saw a number of arrests for fraud and embezzlement, and Wall Street was in for another shock when investment adviser Bernie Madoff was hauled into police custody on December 11. After skulking under the radar for years, Madoff sent the nation gasping when he admitted to headlining a $50 billion Ponzi scheme and concealing millions of dollars in taxes from the IRS.

In the midst of the crisis, the Federal Reserve strode up to the plate, offering emergency loans to banks. This was an effort to keep reputable banks with increasingly shy lenders from collapsing. They established TARP, the Troubled Assets Relief Program, a bank bailout. $250 billion was spent to bail out these institutions, and would later help General Motors, AIG, and homeowners get back on their feet.

Government intervention to revive the economy eventually proved at least partially effective, but the burst bubble had done its damage. CNN declared the following year the "Worst Year for Jobs Since '45" in one of its headlines, and 2008 alone saw the axing of 2.6 million jobs, equivalent to the total number of jobs there are in states like Maryland, Missouri, and Wisconsin. By 2010, that figure had grown by 5.3 million, and this was only in the United States.

In 2014, a *Los Angeles Times* article celebrated a milestone for the American economy. Though change had been sluggish, the economy had reportedly recovered the millions of jobs lost since the 2008 crash. That said, a 2015 report by the International Labor Organization highlighted the 61 million jobs lost across the world since the 2008 recession, and Director-General Guy Ryder shared his concerns with the global economy. Though the economy in Japan and the United States are on the path to recovery, a number of advanced economies, most notably in Europe, have yet to find their way. Ryder ended his statement by noting, "This means the job crisis is far from over so there is no place for complacency."

Once again, Wall Street's credibility has been put to question by the American public. The Occupy Together movement, a self-proclaimed leaderless organization, took matters into their own hands on September 17, 2011. Through Facebook, Twitter, and other social media mediums, the movement called for an event they named "Occupy Wall Street." Peaceful protesters branched out over the 8 blocks of Wall Street with the Charging Bull as their home base. The crowd was colorful and varied, coming with marching bands and impromptu yoga and Tai Chi classes at the Bowling Green Park to add to the fiery atmosphere.

The protesters rallied for justice against social and economical injustice around the world. Many wanted "corrupt" leaders from financial sectors thrown behind bars. A protester expressed the group's sentiments to a CNN reporter: "Something needs to change. We need an economy for the people and by the people, not for the rich and by the rich."

The movement went viral, with many catching on to the trend, including President Obama, celebrities, and even a nod from the cyberactivist group Anonymous. Pizza joints around the country were adding cleverly named "OccuPie" flavors to their menus, and even "Occupy" video games were released.

It was clear – the people wanted change, and they wanted it now.

Chapter 9: Wall Street Bigwigs

"Intelligence without ambition is a bird without wings." – Salvador Dali

Throughout Wall Street's multiple rises and falls, several figures have managed to shove past their counterparts to head the rat race. These key figures have risen to the top at one point in their lives through unmatched ambition and a thirst for success. Some are considered pioneers, and others despicable, but these Wall Street players have made a memorable imprint in the ongoing course of Wall Street's history.

To start off, there was John Pierpont Morgan of JPMorgan Chase Banks. It is a name that rings familiar to many, as it remains one of the largest financial institutions today. In his time, Morgan, the son of a distinguished banker, was the most powerful man on Wall Street. Under his leadership, he merged hundreds of independent factories and railroads to monopolies. But the greatest of his accomplishments came in 1901, when he combined 9 of the most prominent companies to form U.S. Steel. U.S. Steel went on to become the world's first billion-dollar corporation, and was so valuable it kicked up the Dow-Jones Average by 500%. Those around him hailed him as the "King of Corporate Mergers."

J.P. Morgan

Jay Gould was another constantly whispered name in 19th century Wall Street. Only Gould, a

Wall Street Bear, was a name that wrinkled the noses of many, often disgraced as the "Mephistopheles," or the "Devil of Wall Street." Gould was a manipulator, a pundit of the "short sale." This technique involved persuading investors to loan him their shares at a small rate of interest. With the shares in hand, he sold them at the exchange immediately. He would then drag the company's name through the mud, circulating fake rumors through the newspaper he owned. Then, he would buy back the shares at the lowest price possible and return them to the investors, raking in the profits from the difference between selling the spoiled shares and buying them back.

Gould

A modern Wall Street bad boy came in the form of Jordan Belfort. Belfort started his own investment firm, Stratton Oakmont in the 1990s. Together with his partner, Danny Porush, the Quaalude connoisseur swindled millions of dollars from his investors through a pump-and-dump scheme. His brokers thrust flimsy stocks at their clients, which led to stock price inflation. Stratton Oakmont would then dump these stocks, sell off their holdings, and dive head-first into their pool of profits. Belfort was eventually caught, sentenced to 4 years prison, and was personally fined $110 million. His lavish lifestyle of debauchery was captured in the 2013 film *The Wolf of Wall Street*, portrayed by Leonardo Di Caprio.

Jeremiah G. Hamilton was not only one of the very first African-American stock brokers, he is remembered as Wall Street's first black millionaire. At a time when racial prejudice was the norm, his business practices were considered controversial on both sides, as blacks were only expected to do business with other blacks. While he was disliked by many in the industry, he was incessantly made to face the racists that made up most of Wall Street, and he was almost lynched on more than one occasion. At the end of the day, Hamilton had the last laugh. By the time of his death in 1875, he had amassed a fortune of over $2 million ($250 million today), and was declared the richest black man in the United States.

The women of Wall Street, another formerly ignored community, worked tirelessly to climb the ranks. To begin with, there was Abigail Adams. The wife of President John Adams was the earliest documented female investor in the country. President Adams tasked his wife with overseeing the family's farm and finances as he catered to the Revolutionary War. In 1783, Abigail displayed her astute investment tactics when her husband advised her to invest in farmland. Instead, she chose to place her bets on government bonds, which brought her more returns than her husband had even imagined.

Victoria Woodhull and her sister, Tennessee Clafin, were the first women to open their own brokerage firm on Wall Street in 1970. Before that, Woodhull became the first female presidential candidate in 1872. Living in the predominantly male world of Wall Street, the sisters wore custom dress suits to take away from their femininity.

Woodhull

There was also Hetty Green, known today as the "Witch of Wall Street." Green had been under Wall Street's spell ever since she was a child, reading the financial newspaper to her father every morning. Upon her father's death, she inherited an immense fortune, and was one of the few women who had the privilege of managing their own money at the time. By investing in railroads, she quickly became the world's richest woman. In 1898, she even loaned the city of New York $1 million when they were nearing bankruptcy. Despite her riches, she was known for her cheap, crabby composure, and her refusal to let go of her wardrobe of witchy, shabby dresses. At the end of her career, Green was worth a cool $100 million.

In December 1967, Mickie Siebert of Muriel Siebert & Co. became the first woman to purchase a seat on the NYSE. The spunky Siebert was turned down by 9 potential sponsors before finally getting hold of the 2 needed to submit her application. Women across the nation saluted Siebert for breaking down yet another wall for American women.

To complete the list of firsts, there is also Suzanne Shank, the first African-American woman to run a publicly traded financial powerhouse. Shank juggles 2 major responsibilities as the CEO of Siebert Brandford Shank & Co., and in September 2015, Shank also became acting CEO of the Siebert Financial Corporation.

Chapter 10: Conclusion

"Money is power, and you ought to be reasonably ambitious to have it." – Russell Conwell, minister and philanthropist

Wall Street continues to be a prevalent topic of public discussion today, and is one of the most debated subjects between presidential candidates. The amount of research, books, movies, and other creative works the legendary 8 blocks has spawned is in the millions, and that number is still growing. Its history is rife with controversy, complexity, and at times, chaos, but Wall Street continues to remain intrinsic to the global economy, and everyone working there knows it.

There are those who continue to defend it, praising its status for creating what they believe to be the country's most aspirant and intelligent men and women. The adrenaline one gets from the eternal chase on Wall Street is something many breathe for, excelling in a world that necessitates numbers, logic, and rational decisions. Others have labeled those in Wall Street as professional con artists, going by the old saying: "What's good for Wall Street is bad for Main Street." And who can blame them when the current top dogs are making more in one year's salary than the entire GDP of some small nations combined? In 2015, Ken Griffin, founder and CEO of Citadel, made a cheek-slapping $1.7 billion.

The reputation of Wall Street was blemished even more when a study from Canadian forensic psychologist, Robert Hare, came to light in 2012. According to his findings, 1% of the general population is psychopathic, or exhibits tendencies. 10% of that population works in financial industries.

One thing is certain. In spite of its public perception, Wall Street's contentious legacy is a force the world cannot ignore.

Online Resources

Other books about New York City history by Charles River Editors

Other books about Wall Street on Amazon

Bibliography

1. "Stockbroker: Job Description." *Target Jobs*. Target Jobs, LLC, 27 Sept. 2011. Web. 31 May 2016. <https://targetjobs.co.uk/careers-advice/job-descriptions/279111-stockbroker-job-description>.

2. Andrews, Evan. "The Mysterious Wall Street Bombing, 95 Years Ago." *History Channel*. A&E Television Networks, LLC, 14 Sept. 2015. Web. 31 May 2016. <http://www.history.com/news/the-mysterious-wall-street-bombing-95-years-ago>.

3. Beattie, Andrew. "The SEC: A Brief History Of Regulation." *Investopedia*. Investopedia, LLC, 19 Jan. 2013. Web. 31 May 2016. <http://www.investopedia.com/articles/07/secbeginning.asp>.

4. Abraham, Stephan. "The Wall Street Animal Farm: Getting To Know The Lingo."*Investopedia*. Investopedia, LLC, 2 Oct. 2013. Web. 31 May 2016. <http://www.investopedia.com/articles/economics/08/wall-street-lingo.asp>.

5. Beattie, Andrew. "The Birth Of Stock Exchanges." *Investopedia*. Investopedia, LLC, 8 Feb. 2016. Web. 31 May 2016. <http://www.investopedia.com/articles/07/stock-exchange-history.asp>.

6. Macdonald, Chris, PhD. "Wall Street (1987) — "Greed Is Good"." *The Business Ethics Blog*. WordPress, 12 Oct. 2010. Web. 31 May 2016. <https://businessethicsblog.com/2010/10/12/wall-street-1987-greed-is-good/>.

7. Craven, Jackie. "Walking Down Wall Street." *About Home*. About, Inc., 5 Dec. 2015. Web. 31 May 2016. <http://architecture.about.com/od/usa/ss/Wall-Street-Buildings.htm#step6>.

8. Staff, Investopedia. "Where Does the Name "Wall Street" Come From?"*Investopedia*. Investopedia, LLC, 17 Mar. 2013. Web. 1 June 2016. <http://www.investopedia.com/ask/answers/181.asp>.

9. Craven, Jackie. "Architecture of the New York Stock Exchange, the NYSE Building in NYC." *About Home*. About, Inc., 20 Apr. 2016. Web. 1 June 2016. <http://architecture.about.com/od/usa/ss/1903-NYSE-Broad-St-NYC.htm#step9>.

10. Hom, Elaine J. "What Is NASDAQ?" *Business News Daily*. Purch Group, Inc., 9 Nov. 2012. Web. 1 June 2016. <http://www.businessnewsdaily.com/3403-nasdaq.html>.

11. Ro, Sam. "The Shocking Statistic About Psychopaths On Wall Street." *Business Insider*.

Business Insider, Inc., 28 Feb. 2012. Web. 1 June 2016.
<http://www.businessinsider.com/wall-street-psychopaths-2012-2>.

12. NOVA. "The History of Money." *NOVA*. PBS Online, Inc., 26 Oct. 1996. Web. 1 June 2016. <http://www.pbs.org/wgbh/nova/ancient/history-money.html>.

13. Latham, Andrew. "How Much Money Does It Take to Be Considered "rich" in the US?" *Super Money*. Super Money, Inc., 2 May 2016. Web. 1 June 2016. <https://www.supermoney.com/2016/05/much-money-take-considered-rich-us/>.

14. Picardo, Elvis, CFA. "Why Wall Street Is A Key Player In The World's Economy."*Investopedia*. Investopedia, LLC, 24 Oct. 2014. Web. 1 June 2016. <http://www.investopedia.com/articles/investing/100814/wall-streets-enduring-impact-economy.asp>.

15. Polemis, Spyros M. "The History of Greek Shipping." *Greece.Org*. Web. 1 June 2016. <http://www.greece.org/poseidon/work/articles/polemis_one.html>.

16. "2015 Stock Exchange Market Capitalization." *Caproasia Online*. 26 Oct. 2015. Web. 1 June 2016. <http://www.caproasia.com/2015/10/26/2015-stock-exchange-market-capitalization/&gws_rd=cr&ei=gDpVV57KJ6PbmgWfrIf4Cw>.

17. Fitzpatrick, Terry, and Bruce Nash. "Modern Marvels: The Stock Exchange."*Modern Marvels*. Al Roker Productions. 12 Oct. 1997. *Modern Marvels*. Web. <https://www.youtube.com/watch?v=r2JlH5HOjj8>.

18. "The Amazing Origins of the Stock Market We Know Today." *Stock Trading Warrior*. Stock Trading Warrior, Inc., 14 Feb. 2010. Web. 1 June 2016. <http://www.stock-trading-warrior.com/Origins-of-the-Stock-Market.html>.

19. Wood, Cynthia. "THE DUTCH TULIP BUBBLE OF 1637." *Damn Interesting*. Alan Bellows, 16 Mar. 2006. Web. 1 June 2016. <https://www.damninteresting.com/the-dutch-tulip-bubble-of-1637/>.

20. Hayden, Matthew. "5 Economic Collapses More Ridiculous Than This One."*Cracked*. Cracked Media, LLC, 28 Feb. 2010. Web. 1 June 2016. <http://www.cracked.com/article_18397_5-economic-collapses-more-ridiculous-than-this-one.html>

21. Anderson, Jessica Cumberbatch. "How To Keep Tulips Alive In 3 Simple Steps."*Huffpost Home*. TheHuffingtonPost.Com, Inc., 13 Mar. 2015. Web. 1 June 2016. <http://www.huffingtonpost.com/2015/03/13/how-to-keep-tulips-alive_n_6864154.html>.

22. Benjamin, L. S. "South Sea Bubble." *Info Please*. Sandbox Networks, Inc., 2012. Web. 2 June 2016. <http://www.infoplease.com/encyclopedia/history/south-sea-bubble.html>.

23. Colombo, Jesse. "The South Sea Bubble." *The Bubble Bubble*. WordPress, 18 May 2012. Web. 2 June 2016. <http://www.thebubblebubble.com/south-sea-bubble/>.

24. "Blind Pool." *Investopedia*. Investopedia, LLC, 22 Jan. 2013. Web. 2 June 2016. <http://www.investopedia.com/terms/b/blind_pool.asp?layout=infini&v=5B&adtest=5B&ato=3000>.

25. "The Wall Street Crash, 1929." *Eyewitness to History*. Ibis Communications, Inc., 2008. Web. 2 June 2016. <http://www.eyewitnesstohistory.com/crash.htm>.

26. "Philadelphia Merchant's Exchange." *US History.Org*. Independence Hall Association. Web. 2 June 2016. <http://www.ushistory.org/tour/merchants-exchange.htm>

27. "History of the Iconic New York Stock Exchange Building." *Central New York*. WordPress, 26 Mar. 2013. Web. 2 June 2016. <http://www.central-nyc.com/facts-history/history-of-the-iconic-new-york-stock-exchange-building/>.

28. Bellis, Mary. "History of the Stock Ticker." *About Money*. About, Inc. Web. 2 June 2016. <http://inventors.about.com/od/sstartinventions/a/stock_ticker.htm>.

29. Kirkpatrick, Charles D., II. *Technical Analysis: The Complete Resource for Financial Market Technicians*. FT, 2010. *Google Books*. Google, Inc., 8 Nov. 2010. Web. 2 June 2016. <https://books.google.com.tw/books?id=I5SgX5q5sQEC&dq=Edward A Calahan and ticker tape&source=gbs_navlinks_s>.

30. "The Wall Street Journal's First Edition." *Wall Street Journal*. Dow Jones & Co., 8 July 1889. Web. 2 June 2016. <http://wsj.com/125/wsj-first-edition/>.

31. Coe, Taylor. "The Bulls and Bears (and Other Animals) of Wall Street." *Oxford Dictionaries*. Oxford University, 26 Aug. 2014. Web. 2 June 2016. <http://blog.oxforddictionaries.com/2014/08/bulls-bears-business-animals-wall-street/>.

32. Hosey, Anthony Nelson. "Walking amongst Bears and Bulls: The Animals of Wall Street." *University of Valencia*. University of Valencia, 11 Feb. 2016. Web. 2 June 2016. <http://www.uv.es/uvweb/master-banking-quantitative-finance/en/blog/walking-bears-bulls-animals-wall-street-1285952577913/GasetaRecerca.html?id=1285957949203>.

33. Bellows, Alan. "TERROR ON WALL STREET." *Damn Interesting*. Alan Bellows, 15 May 2007. Web. 3 June 2016.

34. Suddath, Claire. "The Crash of 1929." *Time*. Time, Inc., 29 Oct. 2008. Web. 3 June 2016. <http://content.time.com/time/nation/article/0,8599,1854569,00.html>.

35. Leonard, Jonathan Norton. "Three Years Down." *Kirkus*. Kirkus Media, LLC, 20 Oct. 1939. Web. 3 June 2016. <https://www.kirkusreviews.com/book-reviews/jonathan-norton-leonard/three-years-down/>.

36. Griffin, Tren. "A Dozen Things I Have Learned about Investing and Money from Groucho Marx." *25 IQ*. WordPress. Web. 3 June 2016. <https://25iq.com/2016/01/29/a-dozen-things-i-have-learned-about-investing-and-money-from-groucho-marx/>.

37. Terrell, Ellen. "History of the American and NASDAQ Stock Exchanges." *Library of Congress: Business References Services*. NASDAQ/Amex, Oct. 2012. Web. 3 June 2016. <https://www.loc.gov/rr/business/amex/amex.html>.

38. Bartholomew, Joanna, prod. "1929: The Great Crash." *1929: The Great Crash*. BBC. 24 Jan. 2009. *Youtube*. Web. 3 June 2016. <https://www.youtube.com/watch?v=FXNziew6C9A>.

39. Boys, Bowery. "CHARLIE CHAPLIN ON WALL STREET: THE TALE BEHIND THE 1918 PHOTO." *The Bowery Boys: New York City History*. WordPress, 16 Apr. 2014. Web. 3 June 2016. <http://www.boweryboyshistory.com/2014/04/charlie-chaplin-on-wall-street-tale.html>

40. "A Brief History of the Securities and Exchange Commission." *Fox Business*. Fox News Network, LLC, 17 Apr. 2012. Web. 3 June 2016. <http://www.foxbusiness.com/markets/2012/04/17/brief-history-securities-and-exchange-commission.html>.

41. "What Did Women Wear in the 1940s?" *Vintage Dancer*. Vintage Dancer, LLC, 19 Jan. 2011. Web. 3 June 2016. <http://vintagedancer.com/1940s/what-did-women-wear-in-the-1940s/>.

42. Markowitz, Harry M. "The Sveriges Riksbank Prize in Economic Sciences in Memory of Alfred Nobel 1990." *Nobel Prize.Org*. Nobel Media AB 2016. Web. 3 June 2016. <http://www.nobelprize.org/nobel_prizes/economic-sciences/laureates/1990/markowitz-bio.html>.

43. "Technology: The Great Enabler?" *The New Atlantis*. The Center for the Study of Technology and Society, Summer 2003. Web. 3 June 2016. <http://www.thenewatlantis.com/publications/technology-the-great-enabler>.

44. Macalister, Terry. "Background: What Caused the 1970s Oil Price Shock?" *The

Guardian. Guardian News and Media, Ltd., 3 Mar. 2011. Web. 3 June 2016.
<http://www.theguardian.com/environment/2011/mar/03/1970s-oil-price-shock>.

45. Gomstyn, Alice. "When Paper Paralyzed Wall Street: Remembering the 1960s
Paperwork Crisis." *The Alert Investor*. Finra, LLC, 19 Aug. 2015. Web. 3 June 2016.
<https://www.thealertinvestor.com/when-paper-paralyzed-wall-street-remembering-the-
1960s-paperwork-crisis/>.

46. Fernholz, Tim. "The Solution to Wall Street's 1960s Paperwork Crisis Could Also save
Bitcoin." *Quartz*. Quartz Media, LLC, 29 Mar. 2015. Web. 3 June 2016.
<http://qz.com/370553/what-the-cigar-chomping-schleppers-of-1960s-wall-street-mean-
for-bitcoins-future/>.

47. DeVries, Carrie. "Trigger Finger: When Your Finger "Gets Stuck"." *Arthritis-Health*.
VeritasHealth.Com, 28 July 2015. Web. 4 June 2016. <http://www.arthritis-
health.com/blog/trigger-finger-when-your-finger-gets-stuck>.

48. Colombo, Jesse. "Black Monday – the Stock Market Crash of 1987." *The Bubble Bubble*.
WordPress, 3 Aug. 2012. Web. 4 June 2016. <http://www.thebubblebubble.com/1987-
crash/>.

49. Rewiski, Renee. "The Wall Street Bull." *Free Tours By Foot*. Free Tours By Foot. Web.
4 June 2016. <http://www.freetoursbyfoot.com/wall-street-bull/>.

50. Dossena, Tiziano Thomas. "A New York Story How the Charging Bull "chose" Wall
Street." *Bridge Puglia USA*. Bridge Puglia USA. Web. 4 June 2016.
<http://www.bridgepugliausa.it/articolo.asp?id_sez=2&id_cat=37&id_art=3483&lingua=
en>.

51. Wile, Rob. "ANDREW LO: I Read 21 Books About The Financial Crisis And They
Explained Nothing." *Business Insider*. Business Insider, Inc., 6 Feb. 2012. Web. 4 June
2016. <http://www.businessinsider.com/andrew-lo-21-books-financial-crisis-2012-2>.

52. Green, John, and Hank Green. "The 2008 Financial Crisis: Crash Course Economics
#12." *Crash Course*. 21 Oct. 2015. *Youtube*. Web. 4 June 2016.
<https://www.youtube.com/watch?v=GPOv72Awo68>.

53. Amadeo, Kimberly. "Stock Market Crash of 2008." *About Money*. About, Inc., 4 May
2016. Web. 4 June 2016. <http://useconomy.about.com/od/Financial-Crisis/a/Stock-
Market-Crash-2008.htm>.

54. Quinn, James. "Bernard Madoff: How the Scandal Worked." *The Telegraph*. Telegraph
Media Group, Ltd., 9 Jan. 2009. Web. 4 June 2016.

<http://www.telegraph.co.uk/finance/financetopics/bernard-madoff/4277800/Bernard-Madoff-How-the-scandal-worked.html>.

55. Clarke, Tara. "2008 Stock Market Crash Causes and Aftermath." *Money Morning*. Money Morning, 26 June 2015. Web. 4 June 2016. <http://moneymorning.com/2015/06/26/2008-stock-market-crash-causes-and-aftermath/>.

56. Obringer, Lee Ann, and Dave Roos. "How Mortgages Work." *How Stuff Works*. InfoSpace, LLC. Web. 4 June 2016. <http://home.howstuffworks.com/real-estate/buying-home/mortgage2.htm>.

57. Goldman, David. "Worst Year for Jobs since '45." *CNN Money*. Time Warner Company, 9 Jan. 2009. Web. 4 June 2016. <http://money.cnn.com/2009/01/09/news/economy/jobs_december/>.

58. "Unemployment on the Rise over next Five Years as Inequality Persists."*International Labour Organization*. International Labour Organization, 20 Jan. 2015. Web. 4 June 2016. <http://www.ilo.org/global/about-the-ilo/newsroom/news/WCMS_336884/lang--en/index.htm>.

59. Puzzanghera, Jim. "Economy Has Recovered 8.7 Million Jobs Lost in Great Recession." *Los Angeles Times*. Los Angeles Times, 6 June 2014. Web. 4 June 2016. <http://www.latimes.com/business/la-fi-jobs-20140607-story.html>.

60. Pepitone, Julianne. "Hundreds of Protesters Descend to 'Occupy Wall Street'"*CNN Money*. Time Warner Company, 17 Sept. 2011. Web. 4 June 2016. <http://money.cnn.com/2011/09/17/technology/occupy_wall_street/>.

61. Gautney, Heather. "What Is Occupy Wall Street? The History of Leaderless Movements." *The Washington Post*. 10 Oct. 2011. Web. 4 June 2016. <https://www.washingtonpost.com/national/on-leadership/what-is-occupy-wall-street-the-history-of-leaderless-movements/2011/10/10/gIQAwkFjaL_story.html>.

62. Pinola, Melanie. ""Intelligence Without Ambition Is a Bird Without Wings""*Lifehacker*. WordPress, 19 Nov. 2013. Web. 4 June 2016. <http://lifehacker.com/intelligence-without-ambition-is-a-bird-without-wings-1467524135>.

63. Berstein, Iver. *The New York City Draft Riots: Their Significance for American Society and Politics in the Age of the Civil War*. Oxford UP, 1990. *Google Books*. Web. 4 June 2016.

64. La Roche, Julia. "PAST AND PRESENT: The 11 Most Influential Women In Wall Street

History." *Business Insider*. Business Insider, Inc., 29 Dec. 2011. Web. 4 June 2016.
<http://www.businessinsider.com/history-of-wall-street-women-2011-12?op=1>

65. White, Shane. "The Story of Wall Street's First Black Millionaire." *The Atlantic*. The
Atlantic Monthly Group, Inc., 21 Oct. 2015. Web. 4 June 2016.
<http://www.theatlantic.com/business/archive/2015/10/wall-street-first-black-
millionaire/411622/>

66. "A Lil Positivity: Suzanne Shank Is The First Black Woman To Run TRILLION Dollar
Wall Street Financial Firms." *Bossip*. Bossip, 25 Aug. 2015. Web. 4 June 2016.
<http://bossip.com/1207628/a-lil-positivity-suzanna-shank-is-the-first-black-woman-to-
run-trillion-dollar-wall-street-financial-firms/>

67. Montford, Christina. "6 Interesting Things You Didn't Know About 'Black Wall
Street'." *Atlanta Black Star*. Atlanta Black Star, 2 Dec. 2014. Web. 4 June 2016.
<http://atlantablackstar.com/2014/12/02/6-interesting-things-you-didnt-know-about-
black-wall-street/3/>.

68. "Jordan Belfort Biography." *Bio.Com*. A&E Television Networks, LLC. Web. 4 June
2016. <http://www.biography.com/people/jordan-belfort-21329985#the-wolf-of-wall-
street>.

69. Vardi, Nathan. "The Highest-Earning Hedge Fund Managers & Traders." *Forbes*. Forbes
Media, LLC, 24 Feb. 2016. Web. 4 June 2016. <http://www.forbes.com/hedge-fund-
managers/>.

70. "TEN FACTS ABOUT WALL STREET." *Ten Facts About*. Sultana Barbecue, 17 Sept.
2011. Web. 4 June 2016. <http://www.tenfactsabout.co.uk/0029wallstreet.htm>.

71. Mourdoukoutas, Panos. "The Good, The Bad, And The Ugly Side Of Wall
Street."*Forbes*. Forbes Media, LLC, 8 July 2014. Web. 4 June 2016.
<http://www.forbes.com/sites/panosmourdoukoutas/2014/07/08/the-good-the-bad-and-
the-ugly-side-of-wall-street/#6768069a4040>.

72. Pack, Mark. "Did Brokers Really Throw Themselves out of Office Windows in the Wall
Street Crash?" *The Guardian*. Guardian News and Media, Ltd. Web. 4 June 2016.
<http://www.theguardian.com/notesandqueries/query/0,,-1589,00.html>.

73. Rastogi, Nina. "Wall Street Suicides." *Slate*. The Slate Group, LLC, 22 Sept. 2008. Web.
4 June 2016.
<http://www.slate.com/articles/news_and_politics/explainer/2008/09/wall_street_suicide
s.html>.

Made in the USA
Middletown, DE
05 December 2016